It starts with **1 Action.**
One small person
taking one small step
towards **BIG** changes.

It grows to...

THERE IS NO PLANET B!

2 Bold banners

YOU CAN MAKE A DIFFERENCE

People might hold **banners** when they go to a protest, an event where people gather to show they feel strongly about an idea or want something to change.

3 Caring about nature

4 Demonstrating against deforestation

I ROOT for TREES

TREES SAVE LIVES

LEAF Trees ALONE

A **demonstrator** is a person who joins a public protest meeting or march to show that they agree (or disagree) with an idea.

5 Environmentalists

PROTECT WATER

PIPELINE

An **environmentalist** studies nature, especially places where animals, plants and people live. Environmentalists try to protect nature from being harmed by human waste and pollution.

Fridays for Future is a group led by young people who want governments to work harder to fight climate change. It was started in 2018 by 15-year-old Greta Thunberg.

SAVE EARTH

YOU CAN MAKE A DIFFERENCE

SKOLSTREJK FÖR KLIMATET

6 Fighting for our future

7 Growing a movement

WAKE UP
TO CLIMATE CHANGE

A **movement** is a group of people who are working together towards a goal.

8 Healthy habitats

A **habitat** is the home or environment where a plant or animal lives. Habitats can be destroyed when humans cut down trees, pollute water or do other things that harm nature.

9 Inspiring ideas

10 Joining generations

20 Kids for conservation!

Conservation means caring for and protecting our Earth's natural resources, like water, air and trees.

30 Lighting the way

A type of light bulb called LED uses less energy than other types of light bulbs. Using less energy creates less pollution!

40 Mighty marchers

50 Native plants to nurture

Native plants are those that grow naturally in a certain place, instead of being brought there by people. Native plants often use less water than non-native plants and are more helpful for local insects and birds.

60 **O**rganizing ocean cleanups

70 Penguins to protect

Rockhopper penguins are one type of threatened creature. This means that pollution, overfishing and other things humans are doing are making it hard for these penguins to find food and places to live.

Reducing, reusing, recycling!

90

100 Speaking up for science

1,000 One thousand
Testing theories

10,000 Ten thousand
United

100,000 One hundred thousand
Voices raised

1,000,000 One million
Working

10,000,000 Ten million
X-ing out ignorance

100,000,000

One hundred million Youth, including

YOU!

1,000,000,000

One billion

Zooming towards a better future!

It starts with
one small step,
one small action,
and grows...
and grows...

to **BILLIONS** fighting for **BIG** changes.

What Is Activism?

You've just read all about it! **Activism** means trying to make a change in the world for something you believe in. Protecting our planet from climate change is one cause, or reason, why people might become activists. **Climate change** is how the Earth's temperatures and weather patterns change over a long period of time. These changes can make it harder for people, plants and animals to live on Earth. Right now, the climate is changing very quickly and the planet is getting warmer because of human actions such as deforestation and pollution.

People can help protect our planet, but there is only so much that each individual person can do to make a difference. Big businesses (like oil companies) and governments have a lot more power to fight climate change by creating rules and laws that can make a big difference. So actions like recycling and planting trees are important, but it's also our job to make sure our leaders know that climate change matters to us — through activism!

Here are some examples of young activists:

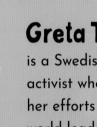
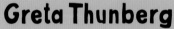

Greta Thunberg is a Swedish environmental activist who is known for her efforts in pressuring world leaders to take immediate steps to fight climate change.

Charles Baldaia is a young climate change expert and activist from Brazil, who speaks up for the rights of his country to be included in meetings between world leaders.

What are some causes or beliefs that you feel strongly about? The next young activist could be **YOU!**

Count Them Up!

Gabriella D'Cruz

is a marine conservationist (an environmentalist who studies oceans) from India. She started a business called The Good Ocean that helps the planet by farming seaweed. Seaweed helps slow down climate change by absorbing carbon dioxide.

1

2

Winona LaDuke

is an Anishinaabe activist, economist and writer. She helped lead the Dakota Access Pipeline protests in 2016, when the American government tried to build an oil pipeline across important water sources on Native land.

PROTECT WATER

PIPELINE

Hans Cosmas Ngoteya

is a filmmaker and photographer from Tanzania. He has founded three different organizations that support and educate local communities about wildlife preservation.

3

4

Jane Goodall

is a scientist from England. She is best known for her lifelong work studying and writing about chimpanzees, which has helped people learn to respect and care about animals. The Jane Goodall Institute works on various conservation projects around the world.

5

Chico Mendes

was a politician and activist from Brazil. He fought to protect the Amazon rainforest from deforestation and stood up for the rights of local communities that depend on the rainforest to survive.

Make It Count!

Did you spot the **9** inspiring ideas?

1 Wind turbines

capture the power of the wind to make electricity. Wind power does not create pollution.

Solar panels

harness the energy in the sun's rays to make electricity. Like wind power, solar power is considered a source of "clean energy."

2

3 Electric cars

help keep the air cleaner as they do not burn fossil fuels like other cars.

Recycling

reduces waste by turning old materials like glass, metal and paper into new items instead of throwing them away.

Walking

4

instead of driving when possible not only reduces air pollution but also helps to improve physical and mental health. Cycling is good too!

5

6 Buses

produce less air pollution by helping people share one ride rather than using lots of cars. So do trains!

7 Planting trees

helps clean the air and make healthy places for people, animals and plants to live.

Rainwater collection

8

is a way of saving the water that falls as rain to use on your plants and vegetables when they need it.

Vegetable gardens

can save money, help you appreciate nature and provide you with healthier food to eat.

9

Count On Us!

Can you help make a difference to climate change? Here's an easy day-by-day guide.

TIP! Make it a family goal to commit to at least one **Count On Us!** day a week. Put a sticker on your calendar when you complete it!

Meat-Free Monday:

If you eat meat, try replacing some of it with vegetables and plant-based proteins. Raising animals for meat uses a lot more land, water and energy than farming plants and beans. You can try replacing or cutting down on dairy too!

Tidy-Up Tuesday:

Are there any areas near you where a lot of junk has built up? With the help of an adult and the right equipment, you could collect some of this to tidy up the nature around you.

Wild Wednesday:

Much of our planet is now covered in human-made things, including buildings and roads. "Wilding" means encouraging nature to come back. Find a local project to get involved in such as planting trees or wildflowers.

Thoughtful Thursday:

Activism can be quiet and careful work. Is there a local leader you could write to about an environmental issue where you live? Or can you find friends who want to help brainstorm ways to take care of the planet?

Fruity Friday:

Try to eat fruit that is grown locally, so it doesn't have to be shipped a long way (which uses a lot of energy). Even better, find out which fruits grow at different times of the year and then try to eat fruits that are in season.

Second-Hand Saturday:

Instead of buying new clothes, books and toys, try finding second-hand things. This helps reduce waste and uses less energy than making new items. When you are done with things that are still in good condition, give them to others instead of throwing them away.

Super Sign Sunday:

Did you spot some good signs and banners in this book? Spend some time creating your own – and then display them for everyone to see! If people ask about your signs, you can talk to them about being an activist.

Author's Note

"Fight for the things that you care about, but do it in a way that will lead others to join you"
— Ruth Bader Ginsberg

I care about the urgent issue of climate change. And I know I'm not alone. But it can be hard to know how exactly we can fight this huge and complicated global problem. What actions can we take that will make a dent? Wondering where to start can feel overwhelming.

But when we join forces, it gets easier. And we can take a cue from Ruth. When we work to inspire others to join the fight, our actions ripple outwards. We create momentum and grow the movement. I also believe we can have more impact when we think about how to put our unique strengths and passions to work fighting climate change. Each person's first steps might look a little different. Will you speak up for science? Nurture native plants? Join conservation efforts? When you take that first step, that first small action, it will grow and grow, leading to BIG change.

— Gabi Snyder

Illustrator's Note

When I was creating the illustrations for this book, I thought a lot about the people who inspire me when it comes to our planet and climate change. My grandfather, David, is one of these people. As a representative for Preston, Connecticut, USA, he was able to create laws so people could recycle their plastics and glass. By working hard on something he really cared about, he made a significant change in his community.

Another person who has always inspired me is Temple Grandin. She is a scientist who studies animals. I saw her speak in person at a lecture when I was first starting as an artist and she blew me away. She thinks about things in such an unusual way and as a result, she's able to come up with amazing ideas about animals and the world. Did you spot her in the book, wearing one of her classic stylish suits? I'll give you a hint. If you find the cow she's pretty close by!

— Sarah Walsh

Photograph by Domestika

YOU CAN MAKE A **DIFFERENCE**

To Violet and Benji,
my nature-loving kids – **G. S.**

To my grandfather, David.
You will never cease to inspire me – **S. W.**

Barefoot Books would like to thank the following people for their help in the creation of this book:

- María-Verónica A. Barnes, Director of Diversity Education, Lexington Montessori School
- Emily Golightly, Media Coordinator / Librarian, Newport Elementary School
- Dr. Adam Wilson, Professor of Geography, Environment & Sustainability, University at Buffalo

Barefoot Books 23 Bradford Street, 2nd Floor, Concord, MA 01742
Barefoot Books, 29/30 Fitzroy Square, London, W1T 6LQ

Text copyright © 2022 by Gabi Snyder
Illustrations copyright © 2022 by Sarah Walsh
The moral rights of Gabi Snyder and Sarah Walsh have been asserted

First published in the United States of America by Barefoot Books, Inc and in Great Britain by Barefoot Books, Ltd in 2022. All rights reserved

Graphic design by Sarah Soldano, Barefoot Books
Edited and art directed by Emma Parkin, Barefoot Books
Reproduction by Bright Arts, Hong Kong
Printed in China
This book was typeset in George, Hugo, Josefin Sans and Might Could Pencil
The illustrations were prepared with a mix of acrylic and water-based gouaches, pencils and a digital touch

Hardback ISBN 978-1-64686-624-3
Paperback ISBN 978-1-64686-625-0
E-book ISBN 978-1-64686-700-4

British Cataloguing-in-Publication Data: a catalogue record for this book is available from the British Library

Library of Congress Cataloging-in-Publication Data is available under LCCN 2022935225

1 3 5 7 9 8 6 4 2

Barefoot Books
Step inside a story

At Barefoot Books, we celebrate art and story that opens the hearts and minds of children from all walks of life, focusing on themes that encourage independence of spirit, enthusiasm for learning and respect for the world's diversity. The welfare of our children is dependent on the welfare of the planet, so we source paper from sustainably managed forests and constantly strive to reduce our environmental impact. Playful, beautiful and created to last a lifetime, our products combine the best of the present with the best of the past to educate our children as the caretakers of tomorrow.

www.barefootbooks.com

Gabi Snyder is a fan of nature walks, wildlife and patterns. Since childhood, she's been especially fascinated by increasing patterns like numbers growing from one to a billion! She lives in the beautiful Willamette Valley region of Oregon, USA, with her family. You can visit Gabi at GabiSnyder.com.

Sarah Walsh has spent the last two decades creating children's book illustrations, large paintings, pattern design, hand lettering and much more. Sarah received her BFA in Graphic Design in upstate New York where she grew up. She currently lives in Kansas City, USA, with her partner, their son and various pets. She works from her plant-filled and sunny studio nearby. Find out more at SarahWalshMakesThings.com.